To:

From:

For this child I prayed.

—1 Samuel 1:27 AMP

Forever My Little Girl

Forever My Little Girl

Loving Your Daughter for Now and for Always

KAREN KINGSBURY

Illustrated by Joanne Lew-Vriethoff

One day a little girl was born into the world, and for a very small moment, her parents held their breath—because that little girl was all theirs, and their hearts had never been so filled with joy.

From her cradle, that baby girl reached up with her tiny hands, took hold of her parents' fingers, and held on tight. And right then her parents knew they would never let her go. Life with that little girl would always mean holding her hand.

Children are a gift from the LORD; babies are a reward.

—Psalm 127:3

Kind heavenly Father,
Thank You for this precious gift—our baby girl.
You have trusted us to care for her.
Now we trust You to guide us.
Amen.

How quickly the baby girl became a one-year-old. She wanted more than just to be held—she wanted to walk.

So she took hold of her daddy's hand, and he led her across the room. And daintily, very daintily, she took her first steps.

From the place where he stood beside her, that father grinned a silly grin . . .

Forever, little girl,
Be my angel, little girl.
Hold tightly to my hand.
Forever, little girl, if you fall, little girl,
I'll always help you stand.

Dear God,

Stay with our little girl always.

Hold her hand and walk with her wherever she goes.

Help us lead her to love You and to trust Jesus as

her Lord and Savior.

Amen.

"I will walk with you and be your God, and you will be my people."

—Leviticus 26:12

For her sixth birthday their little girl got a princess crown. Princesses wore pink satin and curled their hair.

Her father looked at that little princess and took hold of her hand, leading her on a parade around the living room, and proudly, very proudly, that princess giggled at her tall, handsome prince.

And from the place where he marched, that father whispered a quiet whisper . . .

Forever, little girl,
Be my princess, little girl.
Hold tightly to my hand.
Forever, little girl, every day, little girl,
Your wish is my command.

Great Provider,
Thank You so much for Your many blessings.
Help us, as parents, meet our little girl's needs.
Open our eyes to her heart
so that we may guide her in all her ways.
Amen.

And this same God who takes care of me will supply all your needs from his glorious riches, which have been given to us in Christ Jesus.

—Philippians 4:19 NLT

Years passed, and the girl traded her princess dress for a soccer ball.

She pulled her hair back into a ponytail and became a rough-and-tumble soccer player. Her mom and dad took hold of her hands, grabbed her gear, and quickly, very quickly, they jogged with her across the grassy field.

From the place where he ran beside her, that father gave a quiet pep talk . . .

Forever, little girl,

Do your best, little girl.

Hold tightly to my hand.

Forever, little girl, when you play, little girl,

Keep believing that you can.

Heavenly Father,
Bless our daughter with a desire to do her best.
When obstacles stand in her way,
cover her with Your love, protect her, and
give her patience and courage to always keep trying.
Amen.

We also have joy with our troubles, because we know
that these troubles produce patience. And patience
produces character, and character produces hope.

—Romans 5:3–4

Seventh grade came and the girl was changing—now she liked to shop. So she and her mom drove to the mall.

Joyfully, very joyfully, they talked about dresses and makeup and parties and boys. And from her seat in the dressing room, that mom wished a quiet wish . . .

Forever, little girl,
Make good choices, little girl.
Hold tightly to my hand.
Forever, little girl, enjoy today, little girl,
Although your dreams are grand.

Depend on the LORD in whatever you do,
and your plans will succeed.

—Proverbs 16:3

God of all grace,
Please keep our little girl safe.
Protect her from temptation and danger.
Dwell in her heart forever, and always guide her plans.
Amen.

Two more years passed, and the girl was invited to her first dance.

Going to a dance was something she'd dreamed of, but she wasn't sure how to dance with a boy. Her father knew that his girl needed a dance partner to practice with. So he turned on the music, took her hand, and fondly, very fondly, he twirled her around the living room.

From the place where he danced beside her, that father sang a silent song . . .

Forever, little girl,
Dance with me, little girl.
Hold tightly to my hand.
Forever, little girl, when you date, little girl,
Choose as best you can.

To God belong wisdom and power;
counsel and understanding are his.

—Job 12:13 NIV

For wisdom will enter your heart,
and knowledge will be pleasant to your soul.

—Proverbs 2:10 NIV

Blessed are those who find wisdom,
those who gain understanding.

—Proverbs 3:13 NIV

Lord of all,
Guide our girl down a path of right decisions.
Give her the wisdom and maturity to choose wisely,
and lead her into relationships that
are pleasing in Your sight.
Amen.

Seventeen came, and the girl found a crush. Crushes made her parents nervous. Then one day the girl came home in tears because the boy liked someone else.

Her parents knew their little girl's heart was broken, so they took her hand, walked her to the porch swing, and gently, very gently, they made her laugh.

And that mother, from the place where she swung beside her, joked a silly joke. But in her heart her thoughts went like this . . .

Forever, little girl,
Guard your heart, little girl.
Hold tightly to our hands.
Forever, little girl, when you hurt, little girl,
We'll always understand.

The Lord is close to the brokenhearted;
he rescues those whose spirits are crushed.

—Psalm 34:18 NLT

Gentle Savior,

Dry our little girl's tears, and heal her broken heart.

Amen.

The next time the girl fell in love, it was love so real that the boy asked her to be his bride. In the time it took to smile at her ring, her parents' hearts sank to their knees because they knew marriage meant letting her go.

They knew that the walk down the aisle would be the longest of their lives. But her father took her hand, looked long into her eyes, and slowly, very slowly, he walked his little girl toward the front of the church.

From the place where he gave her away, he swallowed a lumpy swallow. But in his heart the words went something like this . . .

Forever, little girl,
Change your name, little girl.
I'll help you take his hand.
Forever, little girl, I'll let go, little girl.
Go have the life you've planned.

"And I will make you my promised bride forever.
I will be good and fair;
I will show you my love and mercy."

—Hosea 2:19

God of all comfort,
We entrust our daughter to You on this new path,
just as we have at every stage of her life.
Take care of our little girl.
Fill her heart with joy overflowing,
and bless her and keep her in the warmth of Your love.
Amen.

A lifetime went by in the blink of an eye, and that father grew tired and old. So old, he shook and trembled and had a hard time seeing his little girl and her man and their three boys. But the father knew where he was going—and he told his girl so—when she sat by his side and started to cry.

The girl took his hand, and lovingly, very lovingly, she told him the difference he'd made in her life. And very barely he squeezed her hand . . .

Forever, little girl,
You will be my little girl.
Hold tightly to my hand.
You're always loved, little girl, you blessed my life, little girl,
More than I ever planned.

Yet I still belong to you;
you hold my right hand.

—Psalm 73:23 NLT

Our precious daughter, in our hearts you'll always be our little girl. At every age and every moment of life, know that you are cherished, prayed over, and oh so loved.

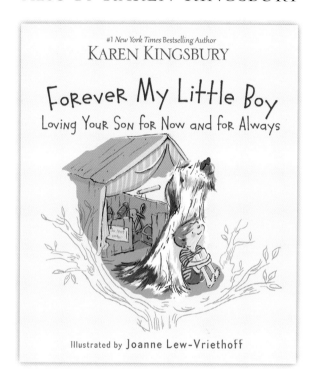

Even when our children grow up,
they always remain our little ones.

About #1 *New York Times* Bestselling Author

KAREN KINGSBURY

Karen Kingsbury, #1 *New York Times* bestselling novelist, is America's favorite inspirational storyteller, with more than 25 million copies of her award-winning books in print. Her last dozen titles have topped bestseller charts, and many of her novels are under development as major motion pictures with Hallmark. She lives in Tennessee with her husband, Don, and their five sons, three of whom are adopted from Haiti. Their actress daughter, Kelsey, lives nearby and is married to Christian recording artist Kyle Kupecky. The couple recently welcomed their first child, Hudson, making Karen and Don grandparents for the first time.